Pieces of Me
Finding Heather Jones

By Tremayne Moore

Published by Maynetre Manuscripts, LLC
Tallahassee, Florida

ISBN Number: 0-985-44638-2 (Paperback)
ISBN Number: 0-985-44639-0 (eBook)
LCCN: 2013912721

Pieces of Me: Finding Heather Jones
Copyright © 2013 Tremayne Moore
www.maynetre.com
Published by Maynetre Manuscripts, LLC
"Writing To Right The Broken Soul"

All rights reserved. Except for use in the case of brief quotations embodied in critical articles and reviews, the reproduction or utilization of this work in whole or part in any form by any electronic, digital, mechanical or other means, now known or hereafter invented, including xerography, photocopying, scanning, recording, or any information storage or retrieval system, is forbidden without written prior permission of the author and publisher, Maynetre Manuscripts, LLC.

The scanning, uploading, and distribution of this book via the Internet or via any other means without permission of the publisher and author is illegal and punishable by law. Purchase only authorized versions of this book, and do not participate in or encourage electronic piracy of copyrighted materials. Your support of the author's rights is appreciated.

This is a work of fiction. Names, characters, places, and incidents are products of the author's imagination, the author's own personal experience, or are used fictitiously and are not to be construed as real. While the author was inspired in part by actual events, the characters are not distantly inspired by any individual known or unknown to the author. Any resemblance to actual events, locales, business establishments, organizations, or persons, living or dead, is entirely coincidental.

The author makes no apology for how the very **REAL** presence of God in this work of fiction may impact the reader's spiritual life.

Printed in the United States of America
First Printing 2013
10 9 8 7 6 5 4 3 2 1

Edited by: Shantae A. Charles, God Ideas, LLC www.shantaecharles.org &
Cynthia M. Lamb, Lamb Editorial Services, LLC www.lambeditorial.webs.com
Cover Design: Robert O. Charles, ROC Studios International, Inc.

Pieces of Me
Finding Heather Jones

By Tremayne Moore

Advance Praise for Pieces of Me & the Writing of Tremayne Moore

"Tremayne is an amazing survivor; his story inspires many in sharing the truth. I am proud to be associated with such a wonderful survivor and advocate." - Lela Albert, Founder of Restoring His People Ministries

"Reading this book induced an overwhelming reaction in me, causing me to pause for composure. This book vividly depicts the unspoken attitudes of abuse within Faith communities. The religious element of abuse is something that many face, but is not talked about enough. I read with tear-filled eyes. Well done indeed!"- Marlanda Yarber, Abuse Survivor

"Refreshing writing style that kept me interested until the very end."
- Lan, Reader

"You are a genius author. I know this journey could not have been easy but what's inside of you to share with the world and the way you share it is needed. Stay in your fight and continue to allow God to use you to bring healing to those who have to bear this heartbreaking cross."-
Melinda Michelle, Author of *Surviving Sunday* and *Color Me Blind*

"Mr. Moore captures the heartbreak of a sexually abused, emotionally deprived child with cunning and aplomb, drawing the reader into the dark abyss of the consequences of dark, demonic abuse. If you have not been abused, your eyes may be opened by the reality of what someone you may know has gone through. If you have been abused, keep the Kleenex close by: you may need it as words, chords, poetry opens up, not the wounds, but the ability to commiserate with a fellow abused person. Weep, if you must, but steady the fight for all that is unjust." Jaci, Reader

Author Foreword & Dedication

One question that many people have asked me is this: "What do you know about domestic abuse?" It's a legitimate question, considering I'm a man, and I have never been in the shoes of a woman who's suffered domestic abuse. During my walk in life, I met a dear friend, and I remember her calling me one day telling me that her man hit her. "WHAT?!" I left my office early to tend to her. She saw me as a dear friend but nothing more, and I was fine with that. I cradled her in my arms and told her this: "if a man hits you, he doesn't deserve you." I meant it then, and I mean it to this day.

A week later, she was supposed to have lunch with me and some friends. She backed out at the last minute, only for me to see her there with the boyfriend who abused her. The feeling I had inside of me made me want to break down and cry. Months later, I would write a poem which would appear in my debut poetry book, "Take It From Me." Of course, I fictionalized the poem, but I wanted to address domestic abuse. If anything, there are men like me out there who care for women who have suffered abuse. And yes, the poem would be the anchor for this book.

Having said all of that, I dedicate this book to every victim of domestic and emotional violence. I also dedicate this book to the families who lost a loved one to domestic and emotional violence.

It's my prayer that all who read this will be willing to take a stand against violent and non-violent abuse.

Tremayne Moore

Courage

Heather held her hands clasped together, to keep from revealing how nervous she was. How much should I tell them? God, please give me strength today. Heather looked into the sea of faces, spotting one, silently encouraging. She could count on Faith Fulbright to be somewhere in the wings rooting her on. She flashed a quick thumbs up as she began to share with the women before her.

"Hi, my name is Heather Jones. I want to share my journey with you, because I want to encourage women who have suffered abuse. There **is** a way to escape. If anything, it's my prayer that my story will make you laugh, cry and cause you to not put yourself in a situation that could possibly cost you your life."

"Today, I've been off and on in this relationship with Marvin Hunter, and we have a son name Jaden. He's currently living in Fort Lauderdale, FL. I'm now living in an apartment in West Palm Beach, FL. I keep telling myself that I'm not going to go back to Fort Lauderdale where Marvin is, but my heart has failed me one time too many. I know he's the father of our son, but I'm scared to go out permanently on my own. I'm surprised that Marvin doesn't know where I am, because he has a tendency to hunt me down or go through my things whether it is at home or at my job."

"I was looking at my life one day feeling a lack of purpose; I started to write about my upbringing to start my road to healing. I'm trying to figure this out, and I'm so thankful to God that I'm still alive. I don't know how I survived the incest and abortion through my early life. Well, let me just tell you what happened."

Sex Escape

Growing up in my family's house was crazy for me. My parents argued at least once a month, and when the arguments were intense, they would get physical with each other. A few times there would come a point where my mother would get a knife to kill my father. I remember one time she chased him down the stairs as he attempted to escape from her. I witnessed once when she chased him with the knife, he jumped out the window and broke his leg. You could smell her anger, like outdated bread, so rancid in her -- I didn't know where it came from at first. As I grew older, I started to understand. That's where I got my strength from. It's funny that I mention my mother's strength, because she was oblivious to the fact that my father was molesting me. I tried to tell her, but she turned a deaf ear. One time I tried to tell her, she got angry at me and threw figurines like a seasoned ball player, nearly taking my head off.

My molestation by my Father started when I was four, and it continued until the time I got pregnant by him, at the age of twelve. It's sad to say my own Father was the Father of the child I was carrying. He threatened to kill me if I told my mother what he did to me and that I was pregnant. So, in order to avoid any beatings from my father, I had to lie to my mother, tell her anything but the truth. *Would I say it was another relative or that it was some neighborhood kid?* Either way, I was known as a pathological liar, and I stayed grounded. Sometimes it would be months to an entire school year. How I was grounded would vary depending on who was grounding me. If it was my father, he would let me off, provided I gave him sex. I learned that sex could get me out of trouble, no matter if it deadened my soul. If it was my mother, it was no makeup, no boyfriends and no phone calls. One time I considered running away from home, but the fear of being on my own prevented that. I didn't understand; I was already on my own, trapped in the abuse.

Let me expound a little bit further about the pregnancy. During that time in school, I went to the school nurse, because I was having extreme headaches and was throwing up. The nurse called my father to have me picked up. He came down, and after the nurse told him what I was dealing with, he smacked me in the face multiple times.

"What you done now? You got the school involved?"

I remember seeing fear in his eyes for the first time. But like a flame from a windblown candle, it quickly disappeared. The sickness continued, and I ended up going to the hospital. I received word that I was three months pregnant. My father demanded that I have an abortion declaring I was too young to care for a child. He was right from that aspect; I was only thirteen years old. I had the abortion for my father, though I wanted to keep my child, and now I'm living with a tear in my uterus. Almost every week, he would ensure that I didn't say a word. My mother was so angry at me and resented the fact that I was pregnant. I was like an embarrassment to the entire neighborhood. I felt the weight of their stares pressing down on me, the mothers barring their daughters from speaking to me or walking on my side of the street, like pregnancy was contagious. I really didn't like them at all. I wanted to tell her that my father was the one who got me pregnant, but my father silenced me and said that some older kid got me pregnant. I don't know if my mother still hates that kid who never got me pregnant to this day. No name was ever given, and strangely, my mom never pressed the matter of meeting this boy.

I actually saw a ray of hope when my father said, "If you get pregnant, you're out of my house." So, I went on a quest to get pregnant; so I could leave. I slept with almost any man I could, some with protected sex and some with unprotected sex. Even through some of those ordeals, I was slapped around during the course of it. I went through it with the mindset of leaving home. The blows became my balm and my path to a way out. I could endure anything except more of what I endured with my father.

I mellowed down once I was pregnant with Jaden. As I think about it, Marvin and I have known each other since third grade. Back then we were like brother and sister, because we were always together, and we had each other's back. Marvin was rarely quiet and a scrawny kid, but he loved to be the neighborhood bully. Now he's near six feet tall, weighing about 250 pounds - most of it muscle. He told me he would always take care of me.

There were times we would walk to school together, and he would carry my books. He was a gentleman at the time. His father wanted him to treat a woman right. During middle school, we dated other people, but it wasn't until our sophomore year in high school when we started dating. I'll never forget; I was homecoming queen in spite of my sordid and well-known history, and he was homecoming king. He was an all-city linebacker, and no one really tried him in arm wrestling or wanted to pick a fight with him. So, at the time, I felt protected with him.

Apart from me cheerleading, my favorite pastime was reading. Whenever I wanted to escape from the pain in my life, I'd read-- erotica books mainly; probably due to what I was exposed to in my life. I guess you could call it self-medicating. Marvin knew I was an avid reader and knew I was into erotica books. I remember reading my first erotica book when I was fifteen. He had no problems with me reading them, considering I was able to learn how to please Marvin (or any man I met before Marvin) by implementing what I read.

I'm sure a lot of people assumed we were dating since middle school, but we were just good friends. Around Christmas of my senior year in high school, I found out that I was near three months pregnant, and yes, Marvin was the father. I had Jaden a month after graduating, and I left home, leaving

Maryland to move with Marvin to Fort Lauderdale, Florida. I was tired of the pain of living at home, and I wanted so desperately to leave not only home, but the state. I just needed a change in my life.

Marvin received a job offer down there, and I was glad I had somebody who brought in a stable paycheck, not like some of these trifling women I knew who were looking for a Baby Daddy. At the time, I saw moving to Florida as a blessing. On the way down to Florida, Marvin proposed to me, and I accepted. So, I was looking forward to starting a future with my fiancé and my newly born son, Jaden. I thought I was finally going to put the past behind me. I thought I finally had a chance to be happy.

A Cult Near You

Once we got situated in Florida, I recommended to Marvin that we started looking for a church, especially for Jaden. We found one less than ten minutes from our new apartment. It didn't take us long to find an apartment, and from the minute we walked in the church, we were embraced by everyone with open arms. The Bishop immediately wanted Marvin to start attending morning Bible studies, and his wife wanted me to immediately get involved with the Women's Ministry.

"We don't want to waste no time! Jesus is soon to come!"

The Bishop was always talking about our "eminent departure." After our first visit, Marvin ran into the Bishop in the grocery store. Marvin always wanted to dress like he was high-class, and that's one thing I'll give him credit for. He could dress really classy, and the Bishop was a classy dresser. Apparently, after the exchange in the grocery store, the Bishop took Marvin on as a spiritual son. My initial thought was that this ministry was only comprised of women, but I would soon learn the Bishop taught the Women studies meetings. Here's the gist of the lessons:

"You are nothing but whores to men, and if you don't submit to your husband, you're in sin!"

It appeared that the focus would be on how we were to treat our men and how to deliver sex to them when they wanted. I was surprised, if not appalled, as to the content of what the Bishop was saying to us. I looked around me, wondering if there was a hidden camera. What was more shocking is that the women were nodding their heads in agreement. After a year of being in this "church," and being brainwashed by this steady stream of male domination and women subordination, Marvin started going through my belongings and questioning who I talked with on the phone. I couldn't believe he had problems with me talking to my mother.

Now I had to ask myself, *what 'church' did I get myself into?* It seemed like I was losing my identity being in this cult posing as a church. Ever since I had given birth to Jaden, Marvin's expectations of how to please him were on a different plane altogether. I would get slapped if he wasn't satisfied with my performance of my wifely duties. As time progressed, I would not even feel like having sex, and I would be lying if didn't tell you that I had thoughts of fooling around with not just men but women too. I didn't give in to those thoughts for the fear that Marvin might consider having a threesome but more importantly, for the fear of losing my life. But I did start flirting with men whenever Marvin wasn't around. It had to be low key.

I noticed my body changing after Jaden was born. My weight was fluctuating and I was starting to have migraines. Because of these changes to my body, I went to have a physical done. A few days after the physical, I had to go back to the doctor, because they wanted to do more tests on me for possible cervical cancer. After the tests, I didn't have cancer after all. I was so relieved, but Marvin decided to ridicule me after the scare by calling me everything but wife, and demanding I clean myself before having sex with him.

Much later, I would discover that was the Bishop's thought of me during the duration of being in the church was that I was simply a piece of flesh to be handled. I'll be honest, during my first visit to the church, something didn't sit right. After about two years, and many threats from the members and Marvin, I left that façade that called itself a church. Marvin stayed there, and truthfully, I wanted to put that experience behind me. I will give Bishop Williams credit; he wanted us to get married, even though it would be on his terms. He told Marvin that I wanted to get married. That's the only one time that the Bishop took my side. All of the other times, he took Marvin's side.

I learned later that the Bishop lied to my face. Marvin told me the Bishop did not have a tolerance for a woman who would not submit to a man. I later discovered he told Marvin to seek and choose a woman in the church who was willing to bow down to Marvin, because that was the pictorial image of the Bishop's marriage. As I look at it now, I'm surprised that Marvin decided to stay with me, but at the same time, his actions were hypocritical. It's like he wanted to implement some teachings when it appealed to him, and disregard other teachings if he could get away with it.

Before I forget, I need to tell you about how a wedding is done in this church we went to. It's only on Sundays after service. Before the wedding, there were to be many dates Marvin and I were to go on which would include the Bishop and his wife… she would monitor our conduct. I knew I had to get out of this cult. If I didn't, I was going to have a breakdown, and didn't want Jaden to see me this way.

Shut Up and Shine

Although I left the church, Marvin allowed me to get a job to bring some extra income into the house. Yes, I said allowed. Having been in that church, it was taught that the wife had to ask permission for *anything* she wanted to do. If she didn't ask permission, she was in sin. It seemed like no matter what I did, I would be in sin. I always thought that salvation was based on faith in God, not on my husband's walk with God. With me taking this job, it stirred up a hornet's nest, and Marvin's abuse increased. He became very watchful of my every move. I was starting to question myself: *why did I even get involved with him? Where was the sweet and shy guy that I knew through our secondary school years?*

Marvin used to tell me everything I wanted to hear, and ever since we stepped foot in that little church, we started having physical altercations. There were times where he would say things that were contradictory, but heaven help me if I were to go back on my words. He would spew things out like,

"In this relationship, you are to submit to everything I say. If you don't, then this house is cursed. It all rests on you. My Bishop backs up everything I'm saying to you. I wear the pants, and so help me God, I will kill you if you look at other men."

I was going to ask about his ex-girlfriends calling for him, but before I could even ask that, he continued on by saying, "I can have relationships with my ex-girlfriends."

It seemed like every day he was having a bad day at work, and he would punch me if the house wasn't cleaned to his standards. I was to maintain a certain figure, wear certain makeup, though my skin couldn't take some products on the market. I was to be his trophy. Shine, but shut up. Look good. Say nothing. Don't change. Be unmoving. When I want to show you off, I'll pull you off the shelf and present you. Until then, shut up, and stay polished. If one snide comment was made behind his back, he'd shove me against the wall and blame me for receiving negative comments. I was a domestic slave. I don't know when I had lost the will to push back, but I had. Marvin admired my attractiveness and hated it at the same time. Women and men would try to get next to me. It was like that before meeting Marvin.

Fixers

I was able to get a much better job about two years later and I worked at this one company as a receptionist. Though the pay wasn't good, it allowed me to breathe while my son was in daycare, and I didn't have to listen to Marvin complain about me all the time. There were two people I met during this course of time that would help me on my journey. One was Faith Fulbright, who is here with me today, the other Charles Johnson.

I met Charles Johnson a week or two after starting work, and he wanted me to call him CJ. He had been with me ever since I started working. Truthfully, I remember seeing CJ in church before I left, but we women couldn't talk to the men without chaperones. When I started my job and first saw him there, I was scared to talk to him. I thought he went off the deep end after I left the church. He was extremely silly, and I thought he needed to be on Ritalin or something to calm him down.

When CJ convinced me that he didn't agree with what Bishop Williams wanted the men to be at the church, and that he had left the church a year ago, I was relieved.

CJ was always sweet to me, but he was a total nerd in my opinion. There were times I would tease him just to see how he would respond to me. Much to my surprise, he actually liked me and wanted to be with me. CJ felt that I could do so much better than Marvin, and he told me he really didn't like how Marvin was treating me. He wanted me to involve the authorities, but I was afraid Marvin would harm CJ.

Something inside me was thinking that even though CJ was sweet, he couldn't please me in bed. Sometimes he would cry when he would see me, and he would console me when he sensed that I was being attacked by Marvin... But Charlie never fully comprehended what I needed in a man. Sure, I attended church, but I still needed a man to give it to me when I wanted and needed it. Self-control was not something I had developed.

"He does all of that to you, but you wish he'd stop treating you like you're a punching bag?"

"CJ, you don't understand--"

"Heather, you have to want wholeness as bad as you want your next breath."

It sounded so cold when I would hear him say it, but I knew deep down inside, it was the truth that I needed to hear. I did want Marvin to stop the beatings and cuttings, but the way my fiancé made me feel sexually kept me with him. I also stayed because I did not want to imagine the thought of my son not seeing his father and all that would entail. He was a good father to my son, and he didn't beat him. I did not realize my actions could shape how my son would see me, as the first woman in his life.

CJ would fix me lunch at times — he was a real good cook. He cared so much about me that he would bring me lunch along with some genetically altered, purple calla lilies. He paid attention to details even my love for purple.

One argument CJ and I always got into was about mental disorders. Looking back, he was actually right. It was almost like he was looking into my life. He said that I might possibly have post-traumatic stress disorder especially after the repeated rape by my Father and the beatings that I was enduring. I had learned to deal with my abuse and block it out when at work. I even went to a therapist once after a short break up with Marvin. I stopped going after one visit because when I went back to Marvin, he told me I didn't need it, and he surely didn't want our business revealed to the public. Besides, I felt I didn't need counseling. CJ was very concerned about it and wasn't ashamed to admit that he was in counseling. He'd say,

"You know Heather, many people don't want to stay in counseling to get fully delivered. And in the church world, we want to claim healing but don't want to see a doctor. Just like our bodies get sick, our brains get sick as well."

I did agree with the therapist when she said that I suffered from post traumatic stress disorder after the incest and the physical abuse, but in all honesty, I was embarrassed that I had to deal with everything that I'd gone through in my life. I did what anyone who's ever been crushed would do — I avoided counseling, even though CJ encouraged me to go, because he cared. He was in therapy as well. Most of his anger was related to authority. Some of his triggers stemmed from living with a narcissistic mother.

I cared for CJ to a point, but now I regret doing that, because he's no longer here. It hurts to lose people once you latch your heart with theirs. At one point, I believed that CJ was asexual. I questioned his sexuality, because when I touched him on the shoulder, he jumped. He did say he was interested in me but because of Marvin, he wouldn't approach me. I felt his respect for me in other ways. It was a first for me. He had been hinting that he would be perfect for me, but I was too blind to see that. We would have arguments over this at times, but CJ felt that neither one of us needed to lose our life over something so petty. He knew Marvin's temper, because CJ came to the church a month before I left and had witnessed Marvin's hostile personality.

CJ tried to keep his distance with Marvin, because he would be blunt and tell him where he could go and how to get there. CJ could come off as preachy at times, but I know he loved the Lord, and he really cared for me.

Truthfully, there are times when I questioned if there was a God. I've heard people say that if a woman is being beaten she's not saved. And at the 'church', they advocated male dominance even in light of unfair treatment.

Another argument broke out between CJ and me when he once called me Dr. Ruth. I initially took offense to it, but honestly, I could see myself as a sex therapist, because I've seen so much of it in my life, done so much of it, and have counseled people on how to handle these type of issues. So, I knew he was right in his observation of me; I just didn't want him to know.

Before the beatings began, sex with Marvin was great. I believe a lot changed after having Jaden and moving to Florida. One thing is for sure: when you are unhappy, you take it with you. You've got to give your soul a clean slate, not just your location.

There were many times when I was apart from Marvin that CJ would invite me to dinner. A few times I'd follow through, but I would always stand him up whenever Marvin wanted some, or when I wanted to stand him up just because. One time CJ backed out of a commitment within the same day, and I jumped on him for doing that. He wanted me to understand that he didn't stand me up like I did him. But I felt entitled, because I'm a woman, and I felt women have the right to do that.

One time CJ became furious after seeing a bruise on my arm. It was the first time I'd really seen him explode.

"What is wrong with you women?" CJ spouted off so many curses in rapid-fire succession, spraying me with his frustration.

"Why are you so adamant *in defending these men who aren't even worthy to have sex with you?"*

I feel so bad not caring about his celibacy and making so many passes at him, God forgive me. My conversations with CJ weren't always heated. Some of our best conversations were about the cult that I went to, which he would eventually leave after a few issues with Bishop Williams. I was felt comfortable talking to CJ.

He sensed that Marvin believed the Bishop was God. Considering the rules of the church, Bishop Williams made it clear men weren't allowed to let women do or buy anything without their consent and approval. The probability of resorting to physical abuse was going to be high, considering the Bishop made it clear that if a woman didn't do what her husband said, even in the smallest detail, they had his permission to slap her. If they didn't, they would be cursed.

Now, I know CJ despised my boyfriend's behavior knowing that he was treating me the way he was. He made it evident the more I talked to him. Of course, Marvin was still at that "church." I may have appeared a bit ditsy, but I was slowly coming around. CJ showed me his notebook, and as I glanced at it, I saw his thoughts. He let me hold onto his notebook for as long as I needed. He said that things got progressively worse after I left. Marvin was still there, and he sensed some tension. I'm sure Marvin believed that CJ was jealous, but they kept their words few among each other.

CJ told me that Marvin was good for butt-kissing; that's how we got the big-screen TV (which he would give back to the Bishop in the hopes that we would receive bigger and better). The things Bishop Williams said were recorded both in Marvin's binder and CJ's binder. Marvin tried to keep his binder hidden, as if it was a secret oath, but I found it and read it. I knew he'd slap me if I read it, but I took that risk. Surprisingly, he didn't. Marvin would smile on Sundays whenever the Bishop called him one of his sons, 'spiritual sons', that is; But a son of what? Of perdition; of abuse; what exactly was Bishop raising up?

CJ noted that, during the Men's Group Study meetings, Bishop Williams always said religions that teach men have "dominion in the marriage arena" have it right. "The man has total control over his wife." He also noted that Bishop made comments saying, when we make a covenant with God, we make a covenant with the spiritual leader. So if we disobey what the Leader says, even if they are wrong, we're sinning against God.

I reflected when Bishop crammed Malachi 2:16 down our throats, and other women in the church agreed that God hates divorce. He said that a woman has no right to leave a relationship. He left out where God says he hates the husband that covers his wife with violence.

The ladies in my Women's Group Study meetings had a plastic façade on in my opinion. They really didn't want to come, because all they heard was that they were to submit. The Bishop taught the Men's Studies and Women's Studies. He would give his role of indoctrination to no one. It was too important to keep the minions in order. His wife was nothing more than a puppet wearing fancy clothes. When he went to work the following day, I snuck and read my boyfriend's Bible Study notes. It read, "God has called me to popularity, and I'm to be the Bishop's right hand man. I will be protected by the Bishop, provided I protect him." Called to popularity? What was Marvin smoking? I can tell you. He was high off of pride. The Bishop was feeding him huge doses of it.

Finding Faith

Faith Fulbright came along right when I doubted whether I could ever find the courage to leave this cycle I was going through with Marvin. After weeks of seeing her coming and going, we finally had lunch together. That lunch rocked me to the core. You see, Faith was the Bishop's first wife.

They had long since divorced, nearly a decade ago, but she helped me to understand a few things. Though I had not shared my past with her, it was almost as though Faith could see beyond my façade and into my heart. Before we could sit down for lunch, Faith gave me a hug. It felt like God himself had reached out of heaven and hugged me. I felt a dam of grief just break inside me. It seemed like every time I had wanted to scream and couldn't, wanted to tell someone what happened to me, wanted someone to believe me, all rolled into one huge waterfall. She just let me cry on her shoulder and soak her cashmere sweater. I think she was wearing my face after that.

"I don't know your story, but pain knows pain, and I have been hurt deeply. It's not your fault, Heather. If you have to tell yourself that three hundred times a day, until you fully believe it, do so. God wants you, and one day, you're going to feel His love pouring into you."

Faith Fulbright gently held me by the shoulders, willing me to look into her eyes. I did. What I saw there was something I couldn't remember seeing since I was a little girl. It was acceptance. She smiled, letting the fullness of her smile light up the room, her coiled hair like rays of energy, her chocolate complexion as flawless as my much lighter skin.

Faith has been in my life ever since, like a gentle wind, pushing me on, and I am thankful for that.

Slap Happy

I remember one night I promised Marvin I'd be home by five, and I walked through the door ten minutes behind. The first words out of his mouth nailed me to the wall; the force of his brutal words cut me and diced me with the expertise of a five-star chef.

"What is wrong with you?"

"I'm cursed because of you, Heather! You stepped outside of your boundaries! I expect you to be home when you say, and keep your word!"

I didn't see the slap coming. It sent me into the cabinet. I was sore for days afterwards. CJ explained to me a day or two later the mentality of an abuser is to know your whereabouts. It's a form of control. If you say you're going to grocery store, but stop by the cleaners, you're covered for the grocery store part of the trip, not for the trip to the cleaners.

The more I think about it, I don't know how many times I had to hear the scripture from Malachi 2:16. Marvin would use it to advocate marriage and remind me that God hates divorce. His belief was that if a man is hitting a woman, she should have no right to divorce. She's to win him over with a quiet spirit. Let God deal with the husband; that's not up to the wife, he warned. I kept thinking *do you really want God to come for you?*

CJ said he was angry when he thought about what he had to listen to during his time at the church. He said there are some women who have been brainwashed into believing that a woman should stay in an abusive relationship, and in his opinion, they need to have their heads examined. If he were to hit a woman, he said he would want to have charges pressed against him.

I remember reading in CJ's notebook where the Bishop said there's a religion that teaches that men are gods. I knew what religion he was talking about, and in our Bible Study he addressed it further to say they shouldn't have backed down to the demands of this country. Religion will always be against government. They got it right, and a man is responsible for a woman – in fact, her salvation hinges on the man. If he screws up, she's screwed.

Turn to that scripture to where it says "you are gods." The Bishop said he was all about male dominance. It's time for men to take over. We have too many single mothers and no fathers stepping up to the plate. We must take our place back in the house, and if necessary, use force!

What a terrible interpretation of that scripture!

I found what CJ wrote about this particular Sunday service to be very interesting. This is what it said... *(Heather looked at the faces of the women, all attentive to what she was revealing.)*

- *Bishop Williams' tolerance has run out for those who haven't made Christ first. There is no close relationship for those who haven't made Christ first.*
- *Pleasing God is pleasing the leadership and a wife's way to please God is to please her husband. He is the head of her life in every way. If we disobey the Bishop, we disobey God. If a wife disobeys her husband, she disobeys God (even if he causes her to sin).*
- *The weight rests on the husband if she cuts up; it's not the wife's fault. She can't do anything that he doesn't allow. So men need to take whatever measure to ensure that your wife does not embarrass you.*

- *Bishop Williams told us that he will drag his wife into his car undressed if she's not ready when he is. God is a God of order.*

- *He mentioned a question that came out of our Bible study. The question was "Can a man help his wife with things inside the house?" The answer? Men are not to be houseboys. That's a woman's responsibility at all times. After reading Titus 2:4-5, he said, men do the outside work, women do the inside work*

- *Proverbs 5 says that a woman's breasts should satisfy her man. So even if your wife doesn't want to have sex, her breasts belong to her man. I know if she doesn't give him what he wants, he can go elsewhere. So women need to satisfy their husbands whether they feel like it or not.*

This was the constant teaching corrupting the minds of those he led and some he still leads today. It is no wonder the congregation has more men than women, especially men who are abusers.

There was one Men's Bible Study that CJ told me about I'll never forget.

"About a month into being in the church, I was ready to leave after the men did an exercise on women anatomy. The foundational scripture was 1 Peter 3:7, and it says for the husbands to dwell with your wives according to knowledge. Bishop Williams said that husbands are to know every part of the woman's reproductive area. No woman should have to teach a man about sex, it's the other way around. Men are to be the master of sex, to teach a woman about what he wants. And because men are to dwell with women according to knowledge, he must know how she wants it. After the bishop said that, he had the audacity to have the men draw a picture of a vagina.

"I sat in disbelief, first because the married men were doing it, and sadly, these men couldn't even draw it. So the bishop had to do it and then asked them how does it open? Again, these men couldn't answer the question. The only question that was going on in my mind was, "What does this have to do with the lesson?" He went on record to say, if he hadn't been behind the pulpit, he'd be a gynecologist.

CJ continued, "Seriously, I questioned the Bishop's sexuality, because he wanted to spend so much time with us, leaving little time for the husbands to spend time with the wives. And I could only imagine when the husbands got home. The wives were to have the dinners prepared and give up some sex. Sometimes we would have certain rituals in our church - such as us men having gun permits. There were times when his teachings would become a bit bizarre.

"Women are here on this earth to give physical bodies to spirit babies. Because of that scripture that said we are gods, women can be goddesses." In his notes, he noted that he asked if women were solely created to be wombs for their use, and the Bishop emphatically said YES! Sunday services were a little lighter, but it was the men's Bible study where it was brutal. We would have our tongues cut if we revealed any of these teachings; we had to be sold out to the Bishop and the 'church' in order to show that we're worthy to learn from the Bishop. But this was so we men can be 'blessed' of God-- Most of the time I could not but wonder what god he referred to."

CJ lost some friends while he was in this cult that posed as a church. As I think about it, I didn't have too many friends during my time there either, and even now, I don't have that many. Marvin got most, if not all, of my time whenever I wasn't at my job.

I'm surprised Marvin didn't threaten my life, because I'm here at this conference. He must've felt, because I'm with women, I'd be safe. Knowing that he's insecure, I assured him I wouldn't reveal anything that's family related. As you can see, I'm sharing this with you, because it's time to be free of the lies and the secrets.

"Girls, do you have a tissue? I need to wipe my eyes."

Heather graciously accepted tissue from another young lady. She knew she was taking a huge risk, but it was time to help someone else avoid her mistakes.

Marvin began to really come against my friendship with CJ, yelling at me one evening:

"Don't talk to CJ no more. I see you've been telling him our business. Are you trying to get me arrested? You're truly outside the will of God, you tramp!"

I expected the slap this time, and I was relieved when he went to his car and drove off. Marvin could tell I was starting to feel free inside, but what was keeping me with him was the fact that he was the father to my son, and that he knew he could please me in bed. The sex is a shallow reason, I know, but it's part of what kept me there.

I also remember one time Marvin and I had friends over, and I was talking to one of my girlfriends. Apparently I was laughing too loud, and Marvin pulled me into another room.

"You're embarrassing me by your laugh. If you don't stop laughing, you won't be laughing after I hit you. If I even think that you're being foolish, I will embarrass you in front of our friends."

By this time, I had no friends – this was a show for him. He was to be the center of attention, and he ran the house.

Patterns

One day, while in the office, CJ was sitting, unusually quiet, not uttering a word; He seemed to be reflecting on life.

"Are you ok?"

"Yes," he mumbled. *I couldn't let it go at that.*

"You can talk to me," I reassured him, putting my hand on his shoulder.

CJ was holding back tears as he started to speak. After taking a deep breath, he confessed:

"Heather, I don't know if you really know me. The reason why I know so much about abuse is because my mother is a narcissist. She was very abusive to my father. I've come to learn that abuse is really about power and control. Even the church we went to was abusive. For one man to have that much power, and to feel that he's not accountable to other men except God, is unacceptable. If I hadn't left home, I probably wouldn't be alive.

"It's something in the brain that causes people to act the way they do. I would like to call it a controlling and manipulative spirit. I don't know if Marvin was abused or witnessed abuse, but if he hasn't, then being at the church surely played a role in Marvin's attitude. Just from the little I've seen in that church, and from what you've shared with me, I can tell that Marvin puts you down a lot. I believe if Marvin wasn't in that church, he'd probably be doing drugs, because his personality resembles a man who's heavy into drugs. Has Marvin ever choked you?"

I answered, "Yes, after Marvin confronted me about talking to you about my relationship. How that came about was I accidentally told him that I ran into you here, and that I had just learned you worked here."

I wondered how CJ would react.

"This had to have been around the time Marvin looked at me devilishly as if he wanted to kill me during a Bible Study meeting when Bishop Williams said to confront your enemies and take no prisoners," CJ pondered out loud.

"Yes, I remember when he came home from work that evening. I asked how his day was, but he could only focus on the Bible Study. He said the lesson was to take no prisoners, and then he mumbled work was fine. He told me he spent the day considering what he was going to do with me, and then he suddenly grabbed me by the neck and said, 'if you ever say another word to CJ, I will kill you.' I thought he was going to kill me right then and there," I said.

"Wow. I'm so sorry that you had to go through that. Have you thought about filing a restraining order?" CJ looked worried. More worried than I had ever seen him before.

I shook my head no to CJ, and I could sense he tried hard not to get upset. So, I told him to continue with his story. He obliged me and continued.

"Most people think that men are the abusers, and it's true. But women can be abusers too. Surprisingly, this is the story of my parent's life. Let me share with you the behavior of my mother and how she treated my father.

"You've probably wondered why I call my mother a narcissist. Let me explain. There were times where I would witness my mother yelling at my father over petty things. Like, if the grass wasn't edged to her liking, she would create a scene out in the neighborhood to prove she was the queen of the hill. He would want the argument to be taken into the house, but she would slap him and tell him she has the right to argue when and where she wanted. She would complain to him that she was sick of him, and she'd mumble under her breath that she was going to leave and take him for everything he had.

"Now, Dad had a well-paying job, making six-figures, but he also had an alcohol problem. One thing that I respected about my father was his belief that – and it is a principle I keep to this day – a man is not to hit a woman, even if she hits him with a frying pan. He'd say the cards will be stacked against a man if he even thinks about defending himself. Hearing that from my dad initially didn't make sense, but as I would get older, I would hear countless stories of men near killing their significant others and giving sorry excuses that they'd change. One story that comes to mind is a man who is lying out the side of his mouth, telling a woman that he'll change and go to counseling, and the woman stays trapped because of her son.

"Maybe this is a bad example, because it sounds like your situation, but I pray that this next part isn't your situation. Some of these men will bite, punch, and drag women from upstairs to downstairs and even injure a woman's spine after throwing her against a wall in front of their kids, but at the same time say that she provoked it. That angers me to the core, but what makes me want to cry is that some of these women will take these sorry men back, hoping they can change a man like this, and the women won't even file a restraining order. And for the church to have the mitigated gall to support the husband and not encourage women to get out of these relationships is a sad indictment. It's even worse outside of our country, but it should not be so here!"

CJ's anger was palpable, his fist clenched, sweat beading on his forehead.

"OK, sorry for displaying my anger, I hope you understand," he exhaled. "Let me continue the story of my parents' relationship."

"It seemed like every time my parents were in an argument my father would grab some gin and juice just to alleviate the inner pain within. The arguments were rather frequent, and his alcohol consumption increased. In fact, his drinking got so bad that he was diagnosed with CPM. That stands for Central Pontine Myelinolysis, and it's caused in conditions of chronic alcoholism, liver disease, and malnutrition. It affects the pons, which is located within the brain stem, damaging functions that control posture, sleeping, eye movement, facial expressions, bladder control, equilibrium, swallowing, dream generation, and respiration rate. Once this area is diseased, the patient will experience severe conditions, which can lead to injury and, ultimately, death. It is not a coincidence that liver disease and malnutrition are also associated with this condition. All of the causes of CPM are causes of alcoholism, which further leads to higher severity of conditions, affecting the midbrain, or the pons.

CJ continued on, "My father wasn't the disciplinarian in the house; that was one of my mother's many roles. It's like my father was to bring home the paycheck, and everything went to her. I know in my family. My parents neglected me, because I was the middle child. The oldest was treated like royalty, the youngest was spoiled, and I was dumped with everything, from chores to being a domestic slave in the house. It wasn't until I was able to attend Florida International University that I was able to leave home.

"Leaving home, to me, signified a long awaited day of freedom. My mother was good at putting on a show, where she was the victim and deserved all the attention. She would go to great lengths to cry, pout and do whatever she could to make people feel guilty; so she could manipulate my father and sometimes me and my siblings. There were times I stood up, only to lose to my father. So, I learned to keep my mouth shut, venting in different ways. I didn't punch holes in the wall or hit people; I'd write or call friends when my mother wasn't around. There was no privacy in the house.

"Before leaving home, there were times when I would listen to my mother's phone calls. She would think I was sleep, when she would be on the phone with her girlfriends. My father was always knocked out early due to his excessive drinking. From calling my father an alcoholic to saying he was a sorry piece of flesh, hatred spewed out of my mother's mouth. I wanted to stand in defense for him, but I knew I would lose.

As I listened to CJ, I realized he wanted to save me from a fate his own father could not escape. He continued:

"Another incident that rang out loud and clear was a month or two before leaving home. I used to write letters and type up some notes to myself on the computer. I would save them on a disk, and if I didn't take the disks with me, my mother would go through them. She wanted to ensure that I was not hurting her image. She wanted to be in every area of my life, either to tear it down or to ensure that her empire was not destroyed. I remember writing a letter to a very good friend of mine, and she pushed me against the wall after going through the trash can to read what I initially wrote. What made it so bad was that I had ripped the letter up; she went through the trash can and taped up the entire letter. What possessed her to do that is a mystery to me. I remember saying that my mother was like a prostitute, because she was always working out, talking about her physique and diet, and ensuring that my father didn't know about the men who came up to her.

"I also wrote that with her attitude of hers it appeared she wanted my father to die. That's why I was pushed against the wall, and then she told my father she was lying on me. And then my father and I got into a fight. Ever since then, I decided to look at my diet, and go to the gym. I needed to defend myself not only against my family, but also for when I stepped out into the real world. I learned that this world was cruel and it's 'every man for himself.'"

CJ leaned over then, staring me in the eyes.

"Heather, I know you tease me, but when I turned seventeen, I was studying my Student Bible, and there was a section that spoke on sex before marriage. So many of my friends were pregnant when I was a freshman in high school; it broke my heart. And because I love God, I didn't want to break not only His heart, but a woman's heart. I care about what God has placed in a woman, and I don't ever want to violate it. Maybe this is why I'm so much harder on men than I am on women."

"One thing my mother tried to do when I was about twelve-years-old was alienate me from all family members. She would tell me horrible things about my father and every member of my family. My uncle, on my father's side, was arrested, and she wanted to make sure that I knew about it. What she failed to tell me was that she was arrested for resisting arrest after being pulled over for speeding. She would tell me that my father was mean, and that he was going to die real soon."

CJ looked sad, regret flashed in his eyes as he continued to pour his heart out to me:

"Truthfully, I love my father, and I'm like him to this day minus the drinking. My mother has told me to stay away from her mother and sister. I used to love confiding in them, and it's sad to know they're not here to see how well I'm doing. When it came down to whose fault it was that my mother's marriage to my father was crumbling, it was everybody's fault except my mother and she has yet to take ANY *responsibility in it. Do I expect her to? Nope. Today, I have learned to trust the Lord and not lean on my own understanding. There are some things I will never understand until I see the Lord face-to-face. So, I've learned to rest in Him."*

"Mom once told me when I was about fifteen, 'If you don't watch your behavior, you're going to be put out of the house. You need to be like your father, and keep your mouth shut when I speak.' If only she knew that she was aiding my father in his drinking. I would stand up to my mother at times. I was sick of her having tirades just because she felt she could have one. My father would want me to back down, because she was my mother. So I would back down to avoid getting into a fight with him, especially with alcohol always in his bloodstream.

"My mother would always yell and lecture me on why I was wrong. She is great at taking events and twisting them around to where I am wrong and not her. She would tell me that what I remember is not how it happened, and then tell me her version of what "really happened." I wish I had recorded everything she would say, it would surely make great dinner conversations. When I would argue back, she would say "that's not true" or laugh at me and tell me how stupid she thought I was.

As I listened to CJ, he seemed to make my problems seem like nothing. He had experienced so much pain. Maybe that's why we were drawn to each other. He went on.

"One time she took the shelf that my stereo was on and forced it onto the ground, damaging it, and then she took my hammer and started damaging my tapes and CDs. If I wasn't crazier, I would've choked her and tried to kill her. There were many times where I wanted to let her know how I felt by choking her to death, but I knew that I would serve a prison sentence, my father would have killed me, and that I would be judged by God if I had done that. I tell you, these emotions still ring throughout my being, and that's why I'm in counseling today."

"So, what are you in counseling for, mainly?" I asked.

"I'll admit it to you, Heather, that I have post-traumatic stress disorder. It's sad that the African-American community looks at mental illnesses, whether it be Bipolar, PTSD, BPD, Schizophrenia and the likes, as a "little black secret" if not a "dirty black secret." My thought on why it's a secret is because of pride or feeling we have something to prove to the world, like we're the perfect family, or my family is better than yours. Just comparing ourselves to others and for what purpose; to insult other people? They didn't do anything wrong. What people need to understand is that people acquire these disorders not by their choice. Abuse or trauma that they didn't subscribe to occurred in their lives. Most parents of children who have any one of those will be the first to deny and say "there's nothing wrong with my child" and will want to curse the doctors, nurses or even educators out.

"If the truth is hidden, and no help is given, we as a culture will continue to perpetuate the cycle of mental illness as well as denial. It's time that we stand up and sound the alarm. In order to be free from mental illness, you must face it head on, and get help for it. It won't go away overnight. The true safe place is in the Word of God. The Lord our God placed doctors on this earth, because we – as fragile humans – get sick. I have my own struggles, and I don't have many friends. People think I'm supposed to be happy all the time, and to be honest, I struggle with life, because most of the time I'm by myself."

I wanted to tell CJ that he had a friend in me, but Marvin was crazy, and if word got back to Marvin, he would flip out. So I kept silent. I didn't want to give CJ any false hopes that I would always be around. Still, I listened.

"Looking at my life now, I can see why I have such a heart for defending those who are weak and who don't have a voice. "My desire is for them to be strengthened by the Lord and to be able to find their voice and let it be heard. I have a story to tell, and Heather, you have a story to share. I believe it will happen once you leave this idiot! I believe my mother is probably bipolar or has a case of obsessive-compulsive disorder, better known as OCD. But of course, this is my opinion. Don't get me wrong Heather, I do love my mother, I just don't like her actions and attitude. Back then, I really hated my mother and wanted her to die. But that was eating me up inside, primarily because it wasn't going to happen. I believe many marriages today fail due to lack of communication and respect. Mutual respect is what's needed more than communication. When one person wants to dominate over the other, no one comes out as the winner. I hated seeing my Father looking defeated and losing at love every day."

"We don't want to admit we need help. It's gotten so bad that when we do find out that we have a disorder, we only go to counseling one time, and then we say that we are cured. Of course, you're lying to yourself about being fully healed... People get cured from the abusive relationship, but if there was molestation from early childhood, that needs to be cured before the abuse. Great therapy comes from finding out the root issue and then determining which one is major and needs to be healed first. If the root issue isn't dealt with, people will perpetuate the cycle of whatever symptoms they are suffering from - they will continue abusing others or themselves remain abused. Jesus is the Healer and He gives the wisdom to deal with the deep issues of abuse in us."

Just as I wondered where the conversation was heading, CJ answered my thoughts.

"How does all of this apply to you, Heather? If you don't go through with a restraining order, I feel in my heart that Marvin is going to kill you. I don't want to sound like a broken record, but I care about you."

"You know, sometimes my mother could get physical with me. She wouldn't do it with my big brother or my little sister, though. If they disobeyed, they would just get grounded. But if I disobeyed, she'd pin me on the ground by my neck call me 'stupid, good for nothing.' She was a physically strong woman, and that could explain why she overpowered my father. My father was relatively quiet and calm. He did not believe in hitting a woman. That's why I have so much respect for him. She constantly punched him, and he only ever hit her once out of self-defense.

"My only resentment was that my father was not as involved as he should've been. He should have had a little more control over his wife. It doesn't matter now; since I'm out of the home. He has to live with her and sleep with her - I don't. I know my father has to live with the guilt of not protecting me. My mother was not all bad, but she left more of a negative impression on me than a positive one, for sure.

CJ had endured a difficult childhood, and yet he had grown to become a wise and kind man. This was clear to me as he continued to share his deepest thoughts.

"When it comes to giving abusers a pass, I believe learning about your history and what we've gone through as African-Americans is not depressing, but letting an abuser get a pass, or those around you letting the abuser get a pass, is depressing. Don't be surprised in the future when Marvin comes to you and says you should both go to counseling. It will be a form of manipulation; so watch out. His words aren't worth anything, and you'll know it's manipulation for real if he drags Jaden into the mix."

Holding Out for a Hero

We had an office function that I missed one Monday. I didn't call in sick, and CJ was worried about me. I was at the hospital.

On the Friday before, Marvin came to my office and surprised me with a bouquet of flowers. That typically wasn't his style, but the card said that he wanted to have dinner with me the following night.

"Get your hair done, and I'll have dinner prepared for you."

He couldn't cook, but after receiving the flowers, I was on top of the world. I was so ecstatic that I jammed to Jill Scott's "He Loves Me" until it was time to see him. I was singing that in the shower, as I put lotion on my body, combed my hair, polished my nails, and even up until it was time to get in the car to go see him. I walked into his house wearing this beautiful, red-satin, strapless dress – and from the look in his eyes, he wanted me to just take it off. We ate dinner first, and then he wanted me to go in the bedroom to light the candles by the bed.

When he came in, everything changed. He pointed a gun towards me and ordered me to take off my clothes and do everything he said. He put the gun down, pinned me down, reached under the bed, and grabbed a rope. He then tied my hands and feet to the bed. He proceeded to rape me and repeatedly punched me in the face. I still have marks on my face from this beating and scars on my arms from the rope.

Marvin had the audacity to leave me tied to the bed while he went out on the town. I'm so glad somebody heard me screaming, and they called the police. An ambulance came, and the paramedics took me to the hospital. Marvin was nowhere to be found.

When I called into the office on Monday afternoon, CJ was determined to speak to me. The office informed him that I had called, and when he called me he immediately asked, what happened? I said "Marvin beat me." CJ said he would be there in fifteen minutes. He came over with some flowers, and he wanted me to just tell him what happened. He was such a gentleman to me. He went into the kitchen and grabbed some ice for my bruises. He told me to lie on his shoulder and cry if I needed to. He kissed my forehead, and I slept in his arms for about 20 minutes. He woke me up and said he needed to leave to ensure Marvin didn't catch him over at the house. I said ok.

That's one moment I'll never forget. I was too blind to see how much of a man CJ really was. He said something to me that I will always remember, and it was this:

"If a man hits you, he doesn't deserve you. When I first met you, you were an angel in my eyes. There really is a bond between us. You may not see it now, but I'm more than willing to wait for you... but don't make me wait too long."

CJ shared something else with me a while ago, but I blew him off. A few years before my beatings got worse, he told me God was speaking to his heart about Marvin. So, he purposely stayed late at work for the next week or two, and he wanted me to go home. I could tell something was bothering him, but I couldn't figure it out. He would not stop crying, and all I kept hearing him play on the stereo was Harold Melvin's "Don't Leave Me This Way." I didn't know if he was attracted to someone and was rejected, or if he didn't want to lose me. I tried to cheer him up by saying, *"you'll find somebody."*

He just looked at me and said, *"You know, I'm sick of hearing that, and I see that as an excuse to say, I'm not perfect for you but a better fit for someone else. Then you pick someone, and they're so trifling that they're not even* worthy to have sex with. I'm tired of living, and it seems like my work is in vain."

I went home at least an hour before him each work day. I was so worried, He had been going through so much for so long, and it felt like he was losing his fight with his mental disorder. I know he was trying to care for my well-being, but I had a strange feeling he had started to become attracted to me emotionally. I didn't realize at the time that pouring our hurts out to each other was making the tie between us stronger and stronger.

Later that afternoon, I was listening to Karyn White's song *"Superwoman,"* and CJ came by my office wondering what was wrong, because he noticed I had repeated the song several times. I tried to lie and say it was nothing, but he was not going to leave my cubicle until I said something. I broke down and told him this song really spoke to how I'd been feeling. I admitted I really wanted to change Marvin.

CJ shook his head sadly.

"Marvin is not going to change. You must be really insane if you think you're going to change him. Marvin is sold out to that cult posing as a church, and as I think about it, there are many people who will put their stock into their church, church leader and their denomination over the Bible. It's a shame. The first person that needs to change is You. You are so special, Heather, and too important to lose. You are not a superwoman. You can't be Marvin's domestic slave. No woman should have to be a slave; so he can run around like he wants and treat you like you're a piece of property. I don't want to sound like a broken record, but I would be less than a man if I didn't tell you this. Granted, if I didn't care, I would sit back and watch you keep getting beat and let you continue on with your drama. You have got to take care of you, Heather. You have got to be here for your Son."

On Impact

Later that night, before going to bed, I was watching the news because of the rain storm that hit our area. There was an accident on I-95, and a truck swerved in and out of a lane and hit a car. Sadly, the car happened to be CJ's car. When the truck hit the car, it caused the car to hit the median and it flipped over. CJ was killed on impact.

I tried not to cry in front of Marvin; so I waited until I went to work the next morning. I knew that was going to be a hard day to work, but to see a letter on my desk from him paralyzed me. He must've stayed late the day before to finish the letter; so I wouldn't see him put it on my desk.

Heather pulled the letter out, unfolded it and straightened it out. It had the wear and tear of being read and cried over many times:

"Dear Heather: you know I think the world of you. This letter might appear prophetic, and I pray that this does not come true for you. I sense in my spirit that something is about to go wrong in your world. I know you can't see it now, but Marvin has you pegged at this point in your life. Because of your association with me, and there being a slim chance of Marvin changing or leaving the church, if you don't get out of the relationship, you won't last another six months alive.

Granted, as I write this letter, I know that my life is also threatened by Marvin. He treats you like property and he feels he's the only one who has access to you. Because of this, either he is going to kill me, or he will hire a hit-man and have me killed. I have prepared for this, and I'm willing to lose my life to try and save yours.

I'm so glad you kept me as your friend, even though you've lost your family and your friends to this poor excuse for a man. I know you still love him, and he satisfies you. I pray that you can rise above the cloud that you're trapped in. The relationship you've been on has been a roller coaster ride, and because you like this ride, it might be difficult for you to get off. One minute you're out of the relationship, and the next minute you kiss and make up.

I know I will never measure up to the man you want. You want a man who will fulfill every sexual fantasy you have. My thought was if you were married and not happy, you'd jump out of the marriage to find someone who will fulfill your fantasies. I don't wish anything bad on you. I wish that I could've been the man for you. I know you teased me, because I was saving myself for the right woman. Granted, I know you didn't care about my celibacy, but I cared everything about you, mind, body, spirit, and soul. We both knew my chances of being in love were slim because I'm mentally sick and not sure what woman wants a man that may need more patience than she can give.

Anyway, my world has faded, and I'm to blame for it all. When you come in tomorrow, I won't be here. I know you're a wounded soul, and I didn't have the heart to tell you, because you would've gotten your boyfriend on me. We both know he never liked me talking to you. If you continue to stay with him, he's going to kill you. I sense that in my spirit when it comes to you.

Heather, you know I love you, and I wish I could give you what you really deserve - that is a man who loves you and is willing to die for you. I don't want to speak death over your life, but I sense in my spirit that you're going to go back to him, and he's going to kill you. I don't wish that for you, and I pray that you get out and stay out of this relationship. Knowing your personality, I know you want to be the center of attention. Why do I suspect with all that you've told me, you are suffering brain damage? But I'm wounded, and I want to be free from this pain.

"You know, people don't care if my dreams die. All they care about is their dream and ensuring it's fulfilled. Once I expressed a dream died, I'm told to get over whatever happens to me. I know I'm going to be considered stupid for taking my life. If no one around me cares if I live or die, why should I? To not belabor this note, the churches I've seen are twiddling their fingers and just going through the motions. We've turned our attention to our own family and tell the world when they're going through a crisis to literally go to hell. I was never felt lovable, and I've always wondered if I would ever be good enough for a woman.

What happened when I decided I wanted to end my life is that only a handful of people didn't give up on me. The tragedy is that we don't feel sorry for those who feel they are at the end of their rope, but let it be someone in their family in the same situation; the world must stop and pray for them. Granted, some could care less if it is someone in their family. If the church is to be the church, but is pointing fingers at those who take their own lives, especially if they know the person's situation, that's a black eye to the faith community.

Men like me will always be brushed aside, because I'm genuine, not trying to toot my own horn. People around me take the side of the woman's arrogance after an abusive relationship – no love, only after what she can gain and uses people, but she'll run swiftly when her world is shattered.

What's true is that people often stay in abusive relationships because of the fear of the unknown, and they return to the relationship, because they are naïve to believe the person has changed or is just feeling sorry. Heather, this is a cycle that has to be broken, and often it must be broken by the person who is subject to the abuse.

As you're reading this, you may be torn inside between your heart and your mind. I hope you remember that I wore my heart on my sleeve, and now I'm making it visible for you to see via this letter. It's a downright tragedy when a man is allowed to hit a woman just because he's the baby's daddy. But heaven help me if I hit a woman. Abuse is abuse, period. And for people to turn a blind eye to abuse, woe unto them. It's time to call a spade "a spade." If battery is a crime, that person, and yes this includes Marvin, must be charged for that crime. Yes, we are to promote love and show love, but a crime was committed.

It breaks my heart that we continue to allow leaders to say they are prophets, and we mere humans exalt them knowing full well they are adulterers and abusers. According to Scripture, they are disqualified, especially if they don't show remorse. It's saddening that these men are seeking women who are virgins to satisfy their own lusts. And we in the church allow the leader to have multiple families in the church. Just know, Heather that God loves women – and they're not doormats. He will judge these wolves in sheep's clothing.

God can do everything that He promised. He can mend your broken heart and soul. And on top of that, He can be a father to your son and not just a boyfriend, but Husband to you. I want you to ask yourself this question: who do you trust? Your church leaders, your boyfriend, or do you trust in God? If it's not God, it's probably because your view of Him was distorted because of the abuse from your father. He was supposed to be a father to you, and he failed you in that respect. It's a shame that there are men who are poor excuses for men, and it blinds you to the good men who are trying to do right. Now when I said that your view of God was distorted due to your childhood, I'm not saying that it was your fault, because it wasn't.

"I'm glad that we both left this particular 'church.' There are many people (men and women) who are enslaved to this type of hoopla in churches today. It's all about me, and what

I can get for myself, without having a heart change for God. People are trying to work their way to heaven, and the truth is they're miserable inside. One day, people's facades of 'I'm happy, and I love the life and the church I'm a part of' will be shattered in front of them. I'm not saying that all churches are bad, but people need to be aware of what's going on around them, and more importantly, what teaching they are sitting under.

One thing I've come to learn is that some Church leaders feel they have more rights than the congregation, but not more responsibility. What chance does an abused victim have when church leaders are given a slap on the wrist and turn a blind eye to abuse of any sort? The abused is beaten; the abuser is then rewarded. If the church and society are pointing fingers at abused victims, what chance does the abused have in surviving?

I guess I also better tell you this, before rumors are spread about me. I was forced to quit my job because of my mental disorder and being in counseling. It's sad that they couldn't disparage my work ethic, and other people were spoon-fed when it comes to doing the job. So, they came after me for other reasons. At one point, my boss wanted me to have a medical examination to ensure that I could do my job. It was a setup: if I passed or failed, they were going to terminate me. You know me Heather, I bow down to no bullying, but I will faithfully do my job to the best of my ability.

When you saw me crying earlier today, my girlfriend broke up with me because she wanted me to give in to every desire she had. I wanted marriage, but she wanted to control how I worshiped and felt that I was immature. In short, she didn't respect the fact that I'm in counseling, and she didn't trust that I was trying to do right for her. I sacrificed a lot for her, but it wasn't good enough for her. I've learned that many women aren't satisfied or they want unnecessary drama in their lives. It's probably something I'll never understand.

One thing I'll never understand when it comes to people in counseling is why they feel that they only need one session - I've seen more women do this than men. Then they wreck their lives and other innocent lives – only focusing on themselves. How would this apply to you? You will probably go to counseling just for the present abuse but never address the abuse you suffered from your childhood. Therefore, you'll still walk around with pieces of your heart and life still damaged.

You know that I have so much love and respect for you, and I hope and pray that you'll be healed from everything you suffered in your life. I believe with all of my heart that if a man hits a woman, he doesn't deserve her. My rationale is simply this: if you wouldn't tolerate it from me, why should you tolerate it from any man?

I support any man who's willing to be a backbone to a woman. I can't stand men who won't stand beside the woman they say they love when they're going through something. So many women need a covering, and they need to know they are protected. Some of these men are just downright sorry and need their spines broken. Just because a man can get a woman pregnant doesn't make him a man. If I can't be a backbone for a woman, cover her in prayer and understand what my honey has gone through, then I'm just SORRY! No woman should tolerate that.

As I close this letter to you, know that I love you, and I want to see you bloom forever like I know you are able to. I love you Heather, and I wish you all of God's blessings over your life."

(There was not one dry eye in the room when Heather finished reading the letter to the conference attendees.)

One thing that I loved about Charlie was that he always tried to save me from Marvin, even at the risk of his own life. There were a few times where Marvin threatened Charlie's life for even talking to me; I still did whatever Marvin wanted. I remember CJ jumping in his car to go confront Marvin after he saw me with the black eye. I put in one of the mix CD's that CJ had made for me. I listened to the songs until Jody Watley's song, *"Everything,"* came on. Then I just started to cry. The words summarized everything CJ was to me. I'd give anything to have him here, to hug him and tell him, 'thank you so much for being a friend.' I know Charlie loved me, and I've never experienced a love like that – one who was so willing to die for me. Knowing CJ, he would've said Jesus did that for us. So, I started to evaluate my current situation with Marvin. I think this is where I really had to ask myself: do I want to continue my life like this?

As I think about all that I've said, it's like God is showing me things that I should have seen all along. Marvin reminds me of CJ's mother in that he's ALWAYS right and never wrong. Heaven forbid when something happens; if it does, it is not his fault. If he does wrong, he will turn events around to make it my fault and have Bishop Williams back it up. Ever since we sat under Bishop Williams, Marvin took on his personality. He never talked; he lectured, because he was always right. Marvin was never like this when we dated. We were equal when we dated, but I did see signs of him being spoiled being the baby of his family, and I looked the other way.

Again, ever since being at the church, Marvin was always determined to have his way. Now I know this is a trait of an abusive, controlling man. I now laugh at myself, because I could hear CJ saying the same thing about his mother.

One afternoon, when we were dating, Marvin called me at about three in the afternoon to tell me that we were going out to eat with the Bishop and his wife. Mind you, I was watching our son, because he had a fever, but Marvin didn't care. He demanded that I find someone to watch him, and trying to tell him that I couldn't - because I was taking care of our son - was out the question.

Marvin's anger intensified when we were fifteen minutes late. He blamed me for waiting 'till the last minute to get dressed for the dinner. I should've been more prepared and know every area of Marvin's thoughts. Looking back, Marvin should've put more interest in our son than trying to kiss up to a Bishop who was a narcissist in his own right.

When we got home that night, he wanted the engagement ring back. Now mind you, the ring came from a pawn shop, even though the Bishop wanted him to buy me a more expensive ring. A more expensive ring would have symbolized the financial level of the Bishop, and Marvin was to represent him as a spiritual son. Again, looking back, this was a way to show that without him, I was nothing. I guess I was to be a pampered down princess who was to be part of Marvin's harem.

Never did Marvin apologize for that, and I wasn't expecting one him to; so I gave him back the ring. I was so used to him threatening to leave me, but he knew for a fact that he couldn't resist the sex I was giving to him. And I'm sure Marvin made sure the Bishop didn't know what Marvin and I were doing. In fact, Marvin ensured that he was the golden child to Bishop Williams. And with blind faith, the Bishop took Marvin at his word. Marvin and I knew that if the Bishop found out, an entire Sunday service would have been about Marvin, and how the Bishop bought everything for him, and that I was nothing more than a woman who accepted "hand me down" clothes. Sounds a bit hypocritical doesn't it? I know. I'm bringing the truth out tonight. I guess maybe I should be honest with myself. Sometimes I surprise myself with what I say.

Marvin's apologies were meaningless, the longer I was with him. He would say it, in my opinion, to make himself feel better, but he would still continue to torment me.

Anyway, Marvin eventually would back down and give me the ring back. He knew on some level that he needed me, and I needed him. I think we both were trying to outsmart each other.

My family really didn't like Marvin because of his demeanor. They sensed he was a man with no direction. At the same time, his parents didn't like me because of my past. After his last altercation with me, he was arrested for verbally insulting a waitress while having had too much to drink. He had to do community service, which the Bishop helped him get out of through connections with the police force. Marvin worked for the Bishop, because Marvin could never keep a regular job. He always blamed it on "the man" as to why he couldn't keep a job. He would never own up to the fact that his crappy attitude was at fault!

Unsuccessful Intervention

One time, maybe about a month before I left the church, my mother came to visit us, because she wanted to see her grandson. She noticed that I had a bruise on my left arm. She confronted me about it, and I told her that we were just wrestling with each other for fun. Knowing my mother's intuitiveness, she didn't buy it, and she made it known I needed to leave Marvin and take Jaden with me. I didn't listen. I was determined to stand by my man.

What was that bruise about? I asked him a question during church, and Marvin punched me saying,

"Don't ever ask a question in church, women are to remain silent according to 1 Corinthians. You are to ask me questions at home."

But I knew better. Whatever Marvin said went. I was to have invisible duct tape over my mouth as I walked. When Jaden sensed something was wrong, I was to say,

"Mommy is having a time out, just like you when you get in trouble."

My mother actually confronted Marvin about the hitting, and Marvin said,

"It was an accident, it was my first reaction after she scratched me and it ripped some skin off of my arm. We were wrestling."

My mother yelled back,

"Don't you ever hit my Heather again, even if it's playfully!"

A few days after my mother left, Marvin hit me again, because my mother saw the bruise on my arm. So after that incident, if I was to be around people, I had to be clothed like a Muslim woman; so any bruises that Marvin gave me would not be visible. He tried hard not to hit me in the face, because those bruises could not be covered.

Sometimes I regret even recommending that we go to church. I really had good intentions, because I wanted Jaden to have a better start in life than I did. Ever since going to that church and watching Marvin worship the ground the Bishop walked on, Marvin did everything he could to implement the teachings of the Bishop. One was from Genesis 12, when God told Abram to leave his family. I remember, when I was there, the teaching was that when a man is joined with a woman they are to leave their families. So, women are to cut everyone in their families off. Marvin liked hearing that, because he didn't like my mother. In scripture, it said the man, not the woman, was to leave his family. Leave it up to this Bishop to further twist the Word.

I was actually surprised when he let my mother come down, probably because he knew she would kill him. She took no prisoners, even though she neglected me for that trifling husband of hers. So, whenever I was furious with Marvin, he would say that my father thinks I'm nothing more than a tramp. Part of me now regrets letting Marvin have access to my past life. Maybe that's why he and my father got along so well. I should've left Marvin the moment they became good friends.

That one time I went to the counselor, she told me that it's common for an abuser to isolate one from friends and family. So I'm completely dependent on the one who's abusing me. Although I'm currently not with him – and I need you girls to hold me accountable that I don't go back to him – I'm under so many mental attacks that I'm thinking things I really don't want to think about. In fact, right now, I just want to get back in bed with Marvin. Being without him has made me a bit insane at times... I could be classified as the woman who's "gotta have it, when I want it."

Continuing on, this could actually explain why CJ and Marvin had so much of a dislike for each other. Marvin disliked CJ, because CJ was trying to get the scales to fall from my eyes. And now they are slowly coming off.

CJ disliked Marvin, because in his eyes Marvin was not even a man. To CJ, Marvin was a boy perpetrating manhood and didn't know how to treat a woman. CJ was glad that I had started to fill out the paperwork to put a restraining order against Marvin. I remember CJ coming by my office to ask, *"Did you file it yet?"*

At the time, I said, *"No, but I will before Friday."* He reluctantly said, *"OK."*

I forgot to tell you this, and this happened near the last beating Marvin gave me... One day when I was doing my normal cleaning in the house. Normally, Marvin cleans his bedroom closet and didn't want me to go through it. He had told me that he would clean the closet and said that I had no reason to go in it. I was fearful of what he would do; he had the ability to accuse me of doing something that I actually didn't do.

For years, I always wondered why, but I believe the Lord wanted me to look in the closet this particular day. I was surprised, he had a camera on the closet shelf, and I started to look at some of the DVDs next to it. Marvin had recorded every argument we had in the bedroom, and he had edited the things he did to make it appear that I was the "bad guy." I decided not to say anything. I was heated, but I had to ensure that I calmed down before he came home.

I called my mother and told her about the camera. She was determined that I should immediately pack and move back up to Maryland. Even though being around that pedophile of my father was the last thing I wanted, I didn't say a word and let her talk.

After getting off the phone with my mother, Marvin called me and said that he would be running a little late with the Bishop. Marvin had taken Jaden with him; so Bishop Williams could show him what the 'luxury life' was like – riding in his Rolls Royce. I told him that my mother was coming back to the house again, that she would be there in a couple of hours. That must've set him off, because he shortened the engagement with the Bishop and sped all the way home.

Surprisingly, he didn't make it home, because he was pulled over by the police. He was driving with an expired plate, and was he was caught driving 40 miles over the speed limit. I had to borrow a friend's car to get him from the police station.

Before I went to get him, I grabbed my mother from the airport and then went to get him. Well, I must have pissed him off again by the time I saw him, because when we arrived, he was visibly upset. When Jaden went to hug my mother, Marvin pushed Jaden to the ground and said, "Where's that worthless tramp?" as he looked over my mother searching for me.

My mother said, *"Excuse me!"*

He said, *"Oh, where's Heather? She knows not to show her face, that's why she had you come in!"*

"Actually, I came in to get Jaden. If I had my way, I'd leave your sorry-no-good-self, right here!" she said.

Marvin turned to the desk clerk and said *"Do you see this? I'm a man, and this is how I'm treated!"*

The clerk ignored him, and Jaden looked really ill. My mother asked Marvin if he knew Jaden was sick.

Marvin shrugged and said, *"Oh, I guess that's why he was quiet."*

My mother told Jaden to go outside and that she'd be there shortly. The clerk then told Marvin he was free to go but would have to appear in court the following day.

Visions and Dreams

I was awakened early the following morning to Jaden having nightmares.

"Daddy is after you," he screamed.

I shook him trying to wake him up and said, "It's OK. Mommy is safe." I needed to keep him calm and reassure him we were safe, though inside I knew this wasn't true.

"Mommy, Daddy and that guy were talking bad about you," Jaden said.

"What did they say?" I asked.

He said, *"She's a tramp!"*

"Is that all they said?"

"All I heard was 'you're a tramp!'"

"Don't believe them," I said. *"I'm fine; just like you're fine. We are going to some place safe."*

Jaden gave me such a tight hug that I couldn't help crying in front of him. All he kept saying was, "It's OK Mommy!" After a brief pause, Jaden broke his silence.

"Mommy, Daddy is always talking bad about you. I tell Daddy that I don't like it and he laughs at me. He says Mommy has issues and I have to straighten her out at times."

As I think about it, Marvin does treat me like I'm a little child when I have the nerve to stand up for myself. I promised Jaden that I'd never leave him with Marvin if I could help it. I really don't want to go to court, for they will force me to share custody or give Marvin full custody. And that will be over my dead body.

So, I told my mother that I wasn't moving back to DC. I had enough money saved up, and I found an apartment in West Palm Beach, Florida. I waited for Marvin to head out with Bishop Williams, and I had some co-workers help me move what I needed to take with me. I took Jaden with me. It was a holiday for me but not for Marvin and Bishop Williams. They still had to work on this holiday.

We moved my things in four hours, and I left Marvin a note:

"I have Jaden with me, and I'll bring him down over the weekend. I can't live like this anymore and I filed a restraining order against you this morning. The police saw the marks you left on me, and I told them that I do not want to press charges."

I know there's a lot of tension between Marvin and me now; since I've reconciled with my family and friends. So, I'm glad that I'm not in Florida now; I need this vacation away from my surroundings. After this last beating from Marvin, I had to get out of the relationship.

He must've asked around to find out where at in West Palm Beach I lived. Two days before catching my flight up here to meet with you to put this book together, he came to my apartment at 7:00am. Of course, I was surprised to see him and wondered how he found out where exactly I lived. As soon as I let him in, he punched me in my right eye, and my next door neighbor had to rescue me. Before she came, after punching me in the eye, I remember him punching a hole in the wall and then hitting me in the face. I'm thankful to God I was still conscious for this beating. Typically, I usually pass out or numb myself when he beats me.

The beauty of my next door neighbor is that she's about his height and weight. I knew not to report this to the state because that would give Marvin more of a reason to continue the beatings. And the way this crappy system is set up, it gives Marvin more rights than me. After that incident in my apartment, I made it a point not to take any phone calls or speak to anyone until I came here.

Why did he beat me? He felt that I was his property, and that he was to put me in my place.

Get On the Path and Fight

So, here I am today. If I knew then what I know now, I never would have left Maryland to come to Florida with him. I hate myself for saying this, but Marvin is like a drug to me, sexually, and it's a hard habit to break. Looking back now, I was too blind to see what Marvin was doing to me, and getting this out feels so much better. When I got the job after leaving the church, I was hoping I could save some money in case I needed to leave and take my son with me. As I think about it more, I really wanted to get away from Marvin.

One thing I've learned is that churches will sap you out - especially if they're not focused on Jesus - and church people will make you feel dirty, like you are the devil! People will treat me as if I'm an outcast. They will act as though the abuser and church leaders, who are focused on self, are more important.

I weep, as I think about why I allowed myself to stay in this relationship. I have been robbed of my innocence; so it was easy for me to sacrifice my life for other people. I was always told that I was not important; my vagina is all that I'm worth to a man.

Some of my father's friends were just perverts, and they used to touch me, but not have sexual intercourse with me. He would watch as they touched me, and I dared not to scream nor cry about it, for I'd be slapped.

If you have suffered abuse, please find someone who has gone through it and has broken free. Pray for guidance as to who to connect with and for a church that will comfort broken souls - not a church that says everything is fine or that they don't have struggles.

Being in the dark is painful. The message I want to get out is this: chains have to be broken, you can be set free.

I'm on the path to freedom, and one of my first steps to freedom is to uncover the lies that I believed from my father, my boyfriend and my church. If you are in a church that is promoting male-dominance, there's a strong chance that it's not of God. If it's telling you that a man's god-hood rests on the woman's obedience to his every whim, it's not of God.

To my fellow sisters who have suffered abuse, know this: when you go through pain, suffering or abuse, God allows the anointing to flow in and through you. And it's because of what you've been through – we have been trusted by God to go through this. I must say, He didn't endorse the abuse by any means, because we could "take it."

Why do we hate ourselves to the point that when someone is looking out for us or trying to help us grow, we ridicule them? We need to learn to appreciate the beauty of ourselves and not want each other to stumble. I'm working through my issues, and it's been beyond hard. I fight depression and guilt every day, but I do fight it!

Heather left the podium to a round of applause and a hug from Faith Fulbright who had come with her to be a support. You could hear a woman sitting in the back crying and singing a song containing the words 'Pieces of Me.' Within ten seconds, most of the women along with Heather were holding each other and singing the chorus of the song. They were singing for at least fifteen minutes.

The Cost of One More Chance

Written by Faith Fulbright:

A month after telling this story for the making of this book, Heather decided she wanted to give the relationship one more chance.

Marvin strangled her to death.

He pleaded self-defense, when the truth was, she didn't do anything to him. He was charged with manslaughter.

I'm so saddened by our judicial system. I hope her story will touch anyone who has suffered abuse and will wake people up to the devastation of what abuse of any type can do to a life. Heather's son Jaden is now in the custody of Heather's mother.

My prayer is that Heather is now at peace and reunited with one man who truly did care for her on this earth: CJ.

End Note:

Domestic Violence is a reality that exists within many church-going couples today, and we must address this issue by educating ourselves about the truth of God filled marriages where spouses love, respect and honor each other.

God hates divorce, but He also hates violence between spouses. The husband is to honor his wife, not abuse her, and the same is to be expected of the wife honoring her husband. The scripture says "Husbands love your wives as Christ loves the Church and gave himself for her." It also states "He who loves his wife loves his own body." This speaks so clearly to the fact that men must have a positive and healthy esteem before they can really demonstrate it to their spouse.

Educational awareness of domestic violence should be a part of the Church ministry and should include support groups for victims of domestic violence. Known abusers should be held accountable to their sin and behavior.

The Church needs to be a place where people can find hope, safety, support, love, and healing. Churches are places of praise and worship, where people go seeking a deeper relationship with God. The Church should be a place of unity and of fellowship, where people come together as the body of Christ.

Refuge House Notes
(Special thanks to Jessica Pinto)

It can sometimes be a struggle to articulate the red flags of abuse, because they often look different for different people.

Isolation is often the first manifestation of an abusive relationship. That can look like someone not participating in family or social events or not participating in hobbies as usual.

Physical violence and sexual violence are often the last manifestation of an abusive relationship. The abuser works to gain and maintain power and control over the survivor.

The abuser may not need to use physical or sexual violence to maintain power and control if other abusive behaviors are working such as:

- Extreme jealousy
- Makes accusations
- Breaks, throws, or hits things
- Frequently makes you feel bad about yourself (mocking, name calling, criticizing)
- Threatens you (break-up, physically hurt you, or kill you)
- Pressures or forces you to have sex (rape, sexual violence)
- Pressures or forces you to do anything
- Calls or texts you excessively with messages, tweets, etc. (Spoiler alert: it's not because they love you; it's about control.)

Power and Control Wheel

PHYSICAL VIOLENCE SEXUAL

USING COERCION AND THREATS
Making and/or carrying out threats to do something to hurt her • threatening to leave her, to commit suicide, to report her to welfare • making her drop charges • making her do illegal things.

USING INTIMIDATION
Making her afraid by using looks, actions, gestures • smashing things • destroying her property • abusing pets • displaying weapons.

USING EMOTIONAL ABUSE
Putting her down • making her feel bad about herself • calling her names • making her think she's mad • playing mind games • humiliating her • making her feel guilty.

USING ISOLATION
Controlling what she does, who she sees and talks to, what she reads, where she goes • limiting her outside involvement • using jealousy to justify actions.

MINIMIZING, DENYING AND BLAMING
Making light of the abuse and not taking her concerns about it seriously • saying the abuse didn't happen • shifting responsibility for abusive behaviour • saying she caused it.

USING CHILDREN
Making her feel guilty about the children • using the children to relay messages • using access visits to harass her • threatening to take the children away.

USING PRIVILEGE
Treating her like a servant • making all the big decisions • acting like the master of the castle • being the one to define roles • putting her down because of race, gender or disability.

USING ECONOMIC ABUSE
Preventing her from getting or keeping a job • making her ask for money • giving her an allowance • taking her money • not letting her know about or have access to family income.

POWER AND CONTROL

PHYSICAL VIOLENCE SEXUAL

Adapted from:
Domestic Abuse Intervention Project
Duluth, MN 218/722-4134

Resources:

If you know someone who is suffering emotional or physical abuse, please contact and encourage the victim to contact, the following:

National Domestic Violence Hotline
Assistance is available in English and Spanish with access to more than 170 languages through interpreter services.
Help is available 24 hours, 365 days a year.
1-800-799-SAFE (7233) or TTY 1-800-787-3224
http://www.ndvh.org

Safe Horizon
http://www.safehorizon.org

Refuge House (if you live in Northern FL)
1-800-500-1119 {24-hour hotline]
1-888-956-7273 (Call this number if you are a victim of sexual assault)
http://www.refugehouse.com

The Stalking Resource Center
This service is provided by the National Center for Victims of Crime.

http://www.victimsofcrime.org/our-programs/stalking-resource-center

Book club questions:

1. Why do we tend to brush off women and men who suffer from domestic abuse, emotional abuse, sexual abuse, and suicide?

2. How can we show empathy and compassion to those who have suffered from abuse?

3. What are ways to equip churches about abuse without hindering the mission of the church?

4. How can we help abused victims seek help when women and men are suffering abuse?

5. How can we break the stigma of "the dirty black secret," when mental illness is discovered especially among Blacks?

6. How would you describe Heather's personality? Marvin's personality? CJ's personality?

7. What are steps that women can take to get out of an abusive relationship?

8. How does ongoing abuse make healing nearly impossible?

9. Why do battered partners procrastinate in seeking help?

10. Why do abused victims stay in relationships that are harmful to them?

11. If your friend is experiencing abuse, how can you help her or him through the process?

12. What helpful scriptures can you share with a victim of abuse as encouragement?

13. What practical resources can you share with victims?

Acknowledgements

First and foremost, I would like to thank my Lord and Savior Jesus Christ, for Your love, salvation and for carrying me through this project.

To my mom and sister (and her family) – I love you dearly.

Dad, though you're not here physically; you're here and living in my heart. I know you're proud of me, and that means the world to me.

I want to extend my sincerest gratitude to the following individuals (who have sown into my life):

Robert and Shantae Charles, I thank you for editing this book, the great cover and photos, your prayers, and most importantly your friendship. You both have been with me since my debut book, and your love and support for me has not gone unnoticed. You are truly my brother and sister for life.

Cynthia M. Lamb, I thank you for your contribution to this book as well as proofreading/copyediting it. Your life has touched my life in a special way. Congratulations on your debut poetry book *"Bloom Forever."*

Angelica Henderson, I thank you so much for trusting me in publishing your debut book *"Why Do You Stare."* I'm so proud of you and looking forward to what God has in store for you.

Tamika L. Sims, because of you I have this book. After reading your book *The Plus Factor*, it caused me to extend a poem from my debut book *Take It From Me* into what's now this story. So to you, I owe you a huge thank you. Not only that, I look forward to the day when you, **Ondrea L. Davis** and I can minister hope and healing on the same platform. I pray many blessings over you ladies. #AuthorPower

Makasha Dorsey, I don't know how you can handle someone like me. I hope I have made you proud from the time we've known each other. One day, I will seek your advice on hiring a personal secretary 'cause I sure will need one (smile).

Dr. Lynn Wilder, thank you for the opportunity to speak to your students about *Deaf, Dumb, Blind & Stupid*. Your testimony has touched my heart, and I look forward to reading your book *Unveiling Grace*. God has so much in store for you and your family. Many blessings to you.

Sharon Vice & Tara Laracuente, thank you for allowing me to pick your brains during the course of this project. **Michele Lax**, thank you for providing the medical research needed for this project.

A special thanks to **Jessica Pinto** and **Refuge House, Tallahassee, FL** for their assistance with research and the awareness and services they provide to domestic violence victims. I also need to thank **Marlanda Yarber**, **Maxine Browne** and **Lela Albert** for test reading *Pieces of Me* and provided constructive feedback.

I would like to extend my appreciation and love to all of the ministries, church families, public and private schools, bookstores, book clubs and different outlets that have supported my ministry.

I would like to extend a special thanks to the ladies of **APOOO Books, Sisters of Ruth Book Club, OOSA Online Book Club, AAMBC** (African Americans On The Move Book Club), **Foresight Literary Lounge,** the **Building Relationship around Books Book Club** (B.R.A.B.), **Barbara Morgan** and **Tiffany Craig** (Tiffany Talks Books) for welcoming *Deaf, Dumb, Blind and Stupid* with open arms.

To **LaShaunda Hoffman** (from Shades of Romance Magazine), **Pure Artistry Literary Café, Paulette Harper-Johnson, Vanessa Richardson & Adrienna Turner** (from The Certain Ones Magazine), **Tyora Moody, Dyphia Blount, Lovey Shareese** and **H.D. Campbell**, thank you so much for the love, support, interviews and promoting my brand.

To all who have been touched by *Deaf, Dumb, Blind & Stupid*, and the *You Can Take It* Series, just know that I love you dearly and we're family. I've got your back, and you will always have a friend in me.

To all of the wonderful authors I have met over the years, I am forever in debt to you. Thank you for sharing your wealth of knowledge with me, and I pray much success in your careers.

To the Tallahassee Authors Network (TAN) family and the Tallahassee Writers Association (TWA) family, you are truly my brothers and sisters in writing (I would thank you all individually; there are too many of you and don't want to miss any of you – smile). The best is yet to come for all of us.

To all of my friends (past, present and future), know that I love you with all of my heart, and you are not forgotten. If I forgot to mention you by name, forgive me; I'm getting old (smile)! Charge it to my head and not my heart.

About The Author

Tremayne Moore, founder of Maynetre Manuscripts, LLC, is an accountant, writer, psalmist, modern-day Griot, and Spoken Word motivational speaker. He is the author of the poetry series *"You Can Take It"* and the novel "Deaf, Dumb, Blind & Stupid." Academically, he holds a Bachelor of Science Degree in Accounting from Florida Agricultural & Mechanical University and a Bachelor of Science Degree in Management Information Systems from Florida State University.

Tremayne's life can be summarized with a quote from the Apostle Paul from the Book of Philippians:

"Christ shall be magnified in my body; whether by life or by death."

☙ ❖ ❧

Publishing Inquiries & Speaking Engagements:
Maynetre Manuscripts, LLC
P.O. Box 14823, Tallahassee, FL 32317

Connect with Tremayne Online:
Website: www.maynetre.com
Blog: http://mayneman.blogspot.com
Facebook: http://www.facebook.com/AuthorTremayneMoore
Twitter: http://twitter.com/Mayntre
Email: tremayne_moore@yahoo.com

Friend to Friend Action Plan
(Proverbs 27:17)

From this day forth, I make a commitment to not be silent or keep silent. I will report, I will warn, I will lend an ear to those who have been abused. I will do what is in my power to help and not further harm victim of abuse.

Ways I Can Help:

1. _____
2. _____
3. _____

My Accountable Friend _____

My Signature_____

www.ingramcontent.com/pod-product-compliance
Lightning Source LLC
Chambersburg PA
CBHW031421040426
42444CB00005B/669